COOKIES & COCKTAILS

CHRONICLE BOOKS
SAN FRANCISCO

Material on pages 6–15, 19–21, and 28–30 previously published in *Very Merry Cookie Party* by Barbara Grunes and Virginia Van Vynckt (text copyright © 2010 by Barbara Grunes and Virginia Van Vynckt and photographs copyright © 2010 by France Ruffenach) by Chronicle Books LLC.

Material on pages 16–18 and 34–37 previously published in *The Christmas Cookie Book* by Lou Seibert Pappas (text copyright © 2000 by Lou Seibert Pappas and photographs copyright © 2000 by Frankie Frankeny) by Chronicle Books LLC.

Material on pages 22–24 previously published in *We Love Madeleines* by Miss Madeleine (text copyright © 2012 by Chronicle Books LLC and photographs copyright © 2012 by Antonis Achilleos) by Chronicle Books LLC.

Material on pages 25–27 and 31–33 previously published in *Big Fat Cookies* by Elinor Klivans (text copyright © 2005 by Elinor Klivans and photographs copyright © 2005 by Antonis Achilleos) by Chronicle Books LLC.

Material on page 38 previously published in *Viva Vodka* by W. Park Kerr (photograph copyright © 2006 by Leigh Beisch) by Chronicle Books LLC.

Material on page 39 copyright © 2015 by Chronicle Books LLC.

Material on pages 40–41, 54–55, and 56–57 previously published in *Spice & Ice* by Kara Newman (text copyright © 2009 by Kara Newman and photographs copyright © 2009 by Antonis Achilleos) by Chronicle Books LLC.

Material on pages 42–43, 48–49, and 52–53 previously published in *Hip Sips* by Lucy Brennan (text copyright © 2006 by Lucy Brennan and photographs copyright © 2006 by Sheri Giblin) by Chronicle Books LLC.

Material on pages 44–45, 46–47, and 50–51 previously published in *Viva Vodka* by W. Park Kerr (text copyright © 2006 by The El Paso Chile Company and photographs copyright © 2006 by Leigh Beisch) by Chronicle Books LLC.

Material on pages 58–63 previously published in *Some Like It Hot* by Holly Burrows and Katie Walter (text copyright © 2005 by Holly Burrows and Katie Walter and photographs copyright © 2005 by Maren Caruso) by Chronicle Books LLC.

Library of Congress Cataloging-in-Publication Data available.
ISBN 978-1-4521-4837-3

Manufactured in China

MIX
Paper from responsible sources
FSC
www.fsc.org
FSC™ C008047

Design by Vanessa Dina

10 9 8 7 6 5 4 3 2 1

Chronicle Books LLC
680 Second Street
San Francisco, California 94107
www.chroniclebooks.com

CIN-CIN!!

CHEERS!

SALUTE!

CONTENTS

SUGAR COOKIES

2½ cups [300 g] all-purpose flour

1 tsp baking powder

½ tsp salt

¾ cup [165 g] unsalted butter, at room temperature

1 cup [200 g] granulated sugar

2 eggs

1 tsp lemon or vanilla extract

VANILLA ICING

2 cups [240 g] powdered sugar

1 tsp vanilla extract

4 to 6 Tbsp [60 to 90 ml] heavy cream or milk, or as needed

Food coloring of choice (optional)

Sliced almonds, sprinkles, nonpareils, decorating pens, and/or red candied cherries, cut in half, for decorating

In a medium bowl, whisk together the flour, baking powder, and salt. Set aside.

In a large bowl, with an electric mixer, beat together the butter and granulated sugar on medium speed until light and fluffy, 2 to 3 minutes. Beat in the eggs, one at a time, beating well after each addition, and then beat in the lemon extract. On low speed, beat in the flour mixture until a smooth dough forms.

Gather the dough into a ball, pat into a thick disk, and wrap in plastic wrap. Refrigerate until firm, about 2 hours.

CONT'D

Preheat the oven to 350°F [180°C]. Line two baking sheets with parchment paper.

Place the dough on a lightly floured pastry cloth or board, and roll out ¼ in [6 mm] thick. Using a 4-in [10-cm] cookie cutter, cut out the shapes and, using a spatula, transfer to the prepared baking sheets, spacing them about 1½ in [4 cm] apart. Gather the scraps, reroll, and cut out more shapes.

Bake until faintly golden, 8 to 10 minutes. Let cool on the baking sheets for about 3 minutes, then transfer to wire racks to cool completely.

TO MAKE THE ICING: In the bowl of a food processor, combine the powdered sugar and vanilla. With the machine running, pour the cream through the feed tube, adding just enough liquid to form a smooth, spreadable icing. (To make by hand, sift the powdered sugar into a bowl. Add the vanilla, then whisk in enough cream to make a smooth, spreadable icing.)

If you like, tint the icing lightly by adding a drop or two of food coloring and whisking to color uniformly. If you want the icing to be different colors, divide it into batches and tint each batch with the coloring as desired. Use immediately, or cover tightly and store at room temperature for up to 2 days. (Do not refrigerate.) Whisk briefly before using.

Using a spatula, ice the cookies. While the icing is still moist, decorate the cookies as desired. If using decorating pens, wait until the icing has set to add details to the cookies. Let the icing and decorations completely set.

Store in an airtight container for up to 3 days.

MAKES 24 COOKIES

OLD SALEM MOLASSES GINGER COOKIES

3 cups [360 g] all-purpose flour, plus more as needed

1 tsp baking soda

4 tsp pumpkin pie spice

1 tsp ground ginger

1 cup [270 g] unsulfured molasses, preferably dark (robust)

¼ cup [55 g] vegetable shortening

¼ cup [50 g] firmly packed dark brown sugar

2 Tbsp dark rum or orange juice

Decorating sugar or granulated sugar for sprinkling

In a medium bowl, whisk together the flour, baking soda, pumpkin pie spice, and ginger. Set aside.

In the bowl of an electric mixer, beat together the molasses, shortening, brown sugar, and rum on medium speed until light and fluffy, 2 to 3 minutes. On low speed, add half of the flour mixture and beat just until mixed. Add the remaining flour mixture and beat just until mixed. The dough should be medium-stiff. If it is soft and sticky, add more flour 2 Tbsp at a time.

Divide the dough in half. Pat each half into a thick disk and wrap separately in plastic wrap. Refrigerate until firm, at least 2 hours or up to 1 day.

CONT'D

Preheat the oven to 350°F [180°C]. Lightly grease two baking sheets.

Place one disk of dough on a floured pastry cloth or board, and roll out ¼ in [6 mm] thick. Using a 3-in [7.5-cm] round cookie cutter, cut out the shapes and, using a spatula, transfer to a prepared baking sheet, spacing them about 2 in [5 cm] apart. Sprinkle with decorating sugar. Repeat with the second dough disk. Combine the scraps, reroll, and cut out more shapes.

Bake until just firm to touch, about 10 minutes. The cookies should not brown. Let cool on the baking sheets for 2 minutes, then transfer to wire racks to cool completely.

Store in an airtight container for up to 3 days.

MAKES 20 COOKIES

CANDY CANE COOKIES

1 cup [220 g] unsalted butter, at room temperature

1 cup [120 g] powdered sugar

1 egg

1 tsp almond extract

½ tsp salt

2½ cups [300 g] all-purpose flour

½ tsp red food coloring

¾ cup [150 g] white decorating sugar or granulated sugar

Preheat the oven to 375°F [190°C]. Line two baking sheets with parchment paper.

In the bowl of an electric mixer, beat together the butter and powdered sugar until light and fluffy, 2 to 3 minutes. Beat in the egg, almond extract, and salt. On low speed, gradually beat in the flour until a medium-firm dough forms.

Divide the dough in half. Beat the red food coloring into half of the dough. Blend until the color is evenly mixed throughout the dough.

CONT'D

Pinch off 1 Tbsp of the red dough. Roll between your palms to form a 4-in [10-cm] rope. Pinch off 1 Tbsp of the plain dough and form a 4-in [10-cm] rope. Press the ropes to each other at one end and then twist them together to resemble a striped cane. Shape one end into a hook. Repeat with the remaining dough. As the cookies are shaped, arrange them on the prepared baking sheets, spacing them about ½ in [12 mm] apart.

Bake until just firm when lightly pressed with a fingertip, 8 to 10 minutes. Remove from the oven and sprinkle with the decorating sugar while still hot. Let cool on the baking sheets for 2 minutes, then transfer to wire racks to cool completely.

Store in an airtight container for up to 3 days.

MAKES 42 COOKIES

PISTACHIO CHOCOLATE CRINKLES

3 oz [85 g] unsweetened chocolate

6 Tbsp [85 g] unsalted butter

1 tsp instant coffee or espresso powder

1½ cups [300 g] granulated sugar

3 eggs

1 tsp vanilla extract

1½ cups [180 g] all-purpose flour

1½ tsp baking soda

¼ tsp salt

½ cup [55 g] chopped raw pistachio nuts, plus about 45 raw pistachios

2 Tbsp unsweetened cocoa powder

3 Tbsp powdered sugar

In a heatproof bowl, combine the chocolate, butter, and instant coffee. Place over (not touching) hot water in a saucepan and heat until melted, then stir until blended. Remove the bowl from the heat and stir in the granulated sugar, eggs, and vanilla. Using an electric mixer or a spoon, beat until smooth.

In another bowl, stir together the flour, baking soda, and salt. Add the flour mixture to the chocolate mixture and mix until blended. Stir in the chopped nuts. Cover and chill for 30 minutes, or until firm.

Preheat the oven to 350°F [180°C]. Lightly grease two baking sheets.

CONT'D

In a small bowl, stir together the cocoa powder and powdered sugar.

Roll the dough between your palms into 1-in [2.5-cm] balls, and then roll each ball in the cocoa-sugar mixture. Place on the prepared baking sheets, spacing them about 2 in [5 cm] apart. Top each ball with a pistachio.

Bake one sheet at a time, until firm at the edges but still soft in the center, 8 to 10 minutes. Transfer to wire racks to let cool completely.

Store in an airtight container for up to 5 days.

MAKES 45 COOKIES

MERINGUE SNOWFLAKES

3 egg whites, at room temperature

¼ tsp cream of tartar

1 cup [200 g] granulated sugar

½ tsp clear flavoring extract, such as vanilla, peppermint, almond, lemon, or orange

White decorating sugar or granulated sugar for sprinkling

Edible white glitter (optional) for sprinking

Use your own paper snowflake designs cut from brown paper grocery bags, or use printed snowflake designs from other sources (print them in black or another dark color so they show through baking parchment to provide an outline). For best results, use patterns about 5 in [12 cm] in diameter, with designs that are not too intricate.

Preheat the oven to 200°F [95°C]. Place the snowflake designs on two baking sheets, spacing them at least 1 in [2.5 cm] apart. Lay a sheet of parchment paper over the designs, pressing it smooth and flat.

In the bowl of an electric mixer, beat the egg whites on high speed until foamy. Beat in the cream of tartar. With the mixer still on high speed, add the granulated sugar in a slow, steady stream, and continue to beat until stiff, glossy peaks form, 2 to 3 minutes. Do not overbeat. Beat in the extract.

CONT'D

Spoon half of the meringue into a pastry bag fitted with a ⅜-in [1-cm] round or open star tip. Keep the remaining meringue covered with plastic wrap.

Pipe the meringue onto one of the prepared baking sheets, following the design of the snowflake patterns. Sprinkle with decorating sugar and glitter (if using). Repeat with the remaining meringue to make more snowflakes.

Bake until firm, about 30 minutes. Turn off the oven and leave the meringues in the oven until dry and crisp, at least 3 hours or up to overnight. Carefully peel the parchment paper from the snowflakes.

Store in an airtight container for up to 1 week.

MAKES 12 LARGE MERINGUES

SPICY CHOCOLATE MADELEINES

⅓ cup [40 g] all-purpose flour

1 tsp baking powder

2 Tbsp cocoa powder

¼ tsp ground cinnamon

¼ tsp chipotle seasoning

½ tsp ancho chile powder

2 eggs, at room temperature

⅓ cup [65 g] granulated sugar

⅓ cup [75 g] unsalted butter, melted and cooled

Powdered sugar for sprinkling (optional)

In a small bowl, sift together the flour, baking powder, cocoa powder, and spices and set aside.

In the bowl of an electric mixer fitted with the whisk attachment, whisk together the eggs and granulated sugar until thick and pale, 2 to 4 minutes. Using a spatula, gently fold in the flour mixture, followed by the ⅓ cup [75 g] melted butter, and mix until just combined. Cover with plastic wrap, pressing the wrap directly against the surface to prevent the batter from drying out, and refrigerate for at least 3 hours, or up to 3 days. (This helps develop the characteristic "crown," known as the hump or the bump.)

Preheat the oven to 400°F [200°C]. Generously butter and flour a madeleine pan, tapping out any excess.

CONT'D

23

Spoon or pipe the batter into the prepared pan, filling each mold about three-quarters full. Tap the pan lightly on the counter to remove air bubbles.

Bake until the madeleines lighten and spring back when touched, 11 to 13 minutes. Immediately turn out the madeleines onto a wire rack and let cool completely. When cool, sprinkle with powdered sugar, if desired.

Serve warm or at room temperature. Madeleines are best eaten the same day they are made.

MAKES 12 MADELEINES

JUMBO BLACK-BOTTOM COCONUT MACAROONS

2⅔ cups [200 g] shredded sweetened coconut

½ cup [60 ml] sweetened condensed milk

⅛ tsp salt

1½ tsp almond extract

½ tsp vanilla extract

1 egg white

Pinch of cream of tartar

1 Tbsp sugar

CHOCOLATE COATING

9 oz [255 g] semisweet chocolate, chopped

1 Tbsp canola oil or corn oil

Preheat the oven to 350°F [180°C]. Line a baking sheet with parchment paper and butter the paper.

In a large bowl, use a fork to combine the coconut, condensed milk, salt, almond extract, and vanilla. Set aside.

In an impeccably clean medium bowl, use a whisk or a hand-held mixer on low speed to beat the egg white with the cream of tartar until foamy and the cream of tartar has dissolved. Whisk vigorously or beat on medium-high speed until soft peaks form. Whisk or beat in the sugar. Use a rubber spatula to fold half of the whipped egg white mixture into the coconut mixture, then fold in the remaining egg white mixture.

CONT'D

Using a large ice-cream scoop, scoop scant ¼-cup [40-g] mounds of the coconut batter onto the prepared baking sheet, spacing them about 2 in [5 cm] apart.

Bake until the bottoms of the cookies and the tips of the coconut shreds are light brown, about 17 minutes. Let cool on the baking sheet for 5 minutes, then slide a metal spatula under the macaroons to loosen them from the parchment and transfer to a wire rack to cool completely.

TO MAKE THE CHOCOLATE COATING: Put the chocolate and canola oil in a heatproof container (or the top of a double boiler) and place it over, but not touching, a saucepan of barely simmering water (or the bottom of the double boiler). Stir until the chocolate is melted and smooth. Remove from the heat and let cool and thicken slightly, about 10 minutes.

Scrape the chocolate coating into a small bowl. Dip the bottom of each macaroon in the chocolate and place the cookies, chocolate-bottoms up or on their sides, on the wire rack. (You will have some chocolate coating left over for another use or to pour over ice cream.) Let the macaroons sit at room temperature until the chocolate coating is firm, about 1 hour. Or, to speed the firming of the chocolate, refrigerate the macaroons on the rack for about 15 minutes.

Store in an airtight container in the refrigerator for up to 5 days.

MAKES 10 MACAROONS

PISTACHIO AND CRANBERRY BISCOTTI

3 cups [360 g] all-purpose flour

2 tsp baking powder

½ tsp salt

1 cup [200 g] sugar

3 eggs

¼ cup [55 g] unsalted butter, melted and slightly cooled

1 tsp vanilla extract

½ tsp orange extract

1 cup [110 g] unsalted pistachios, coarsely chopped

1 cup [170 g] dried cranberries, coarsely chopped

Preheat the oven to 350°F [180°C]. Line a large baking sheet with parchment paper.

In a medium bowl, whisk together the flour, baking powder, and salt. Set aside.

In the bowl of an electric mixer, beat together the sugar and eggs on high speed until pale yellow. On medium speed, beat in the butter, vanilla, and orange extract. On low speed, beat in the flour mixture just until mixed. Stir in the pistachios and cranberries. The dough will be medium-stiff.

Spoon the dough onto the prepared baking sheet in two strips, each about 12 in [30.5 cm] long. With wet fingers, pat each strip into a log about 3 in [7.5 cm] wide and taller in the center than at the edges. Refrigerate until firm, about 20 minutes.

CONT'D

Bake until lightly browned and nearly firm to the touch, about 30 minutes. Let cool on the baking sheet on a wire rack for 30 minutes, then carefully transfer the logs to a cutting board, using the parchment to help lift them.

Lower the oven temperature to 325°F [165°C]. Line the baking sheet with fresh parchment paper.

Cut the logs crosswise into ½-in- [12-mm-] thick slices. Place the slices, with a cut side down, on the prepared baking sheet, spacing them about ¼ in [6 mm] apart.

Bake until pale gold, about 20 minutes. Let cool completely on the baking sheet on the wire rack. The biscotti will crisp as they cool.

Store in an airtight container for up to 1 week.

MAKES 40 COOKIES

CHOCOLATE-PEPPERMINT CRUNCH COOKIE BARK

1½ cups [180 g] all-purpose flour

¾ tsp baking soda

½ tsp salt

½ cup [50 g] unsweetened Dutch-process cocoa powder

1 cup [220 g] unsalted butter, melted and cooled slightly

¾ cup [150 g] granulated sugar

½ cup [100 g] firmly packed light brown sugar

2 Tbsp water

2 tsp vanilla extract

3 cups [540 g] semisweet chocolate chips

¾ cup [120 g] crushed peppermint candy

Preheat the oven to 350°F [180°C]. Grease two baking sheets.

In a medium bowl, stir together the flour, baking soda, and salt. Sift the cocoa powder onto the flour mixture and set aside.

In the bowl of an electric mixer, mix the melted butter, granulated sugar, brown sugar, water, and vanilla on low speed until smooth, about 30 seconds. Stop the mixer and scrape the sides of the bowl as needed during mixing. Add the flour mixture, mixing just until incorporated. Stir in 1½ cups [270 g] of the chocolate chips.

CONT'D

Leaving a 3-in [7.5-cm] border on all sides, use a thin metal spatula to spread half of the dough on one baking sheet into a rough rectangle that measures about 11 by 8 in [28 by 20 cm] and is about ¼ in [6 mm] thick. Use the palms of your hands to help pat it into an even layer. Repeat with the remaining dough on the second baking sheet.

Bake one sheet at a time until the top looks dull, not shiny, and feels evenly firm at the edges and center, about 14 minutes. As soon as each baking sheet comes out of the oven, sprinkle half of the remaining chocolate chips over each slab. Let the chocolate chips sit for 5 minutes to soften and melt. When the chips have partially melted, use a small metal spatula to spread them over the cookies, covering most of the cookies. While the chocolate is still warm, sprinkle the peppermint candy evenly over both slabs.

Let cool on the baking sheets on a wire rack until the chocolate topping is firm, about 2 hours. Or, to speed the cooling, cool the cookies on the baking sheets for about 30 minutes, then refrigerate them, still on the baking sheets, just until the chocolate topping firms, then remove from the refrigerator. The cookie bark will become crisp as it cools. Break each cookie slab into about twelve 5- to 6-in- [12- to 15-cm-] long irregular pieces.

Store layered between sheets of wax paper in an airtight container for up to 5 days.

MAKES ABOUT 24 PIECES

CHOCOLATE-PECAN CARAMEL CANDY BARS

CRUST

1½ cups [180 g] all-purpose flour

½ cup [100 g] firmly packed light brown sugar

½ cup [110 g] chilled unsalted butter

1 cup [200 g] firmly packed dark brown sugar

3 Tbsp honey

3 Tbsp heavy cream

2 Tbsp maple syrup

TOPPING

6 Tbsp [85 g] unsalted butter, at room temperature

1½ cups [165 g] chopped pecans or walnuts

½ cup [90 g] semisweet chocolate chips

TO MAKE THE CRUST: Preheat the oven to 350°F [180°C]. Line a 9-by-13-in [23-by-33-cm] baking pan with parchment paper.

In a food processor or in a bowl, combine the flour and light brown sugar and pulse briefly or stir to mix. Add the butter and process or mix until crumbly. Transfer the mixture to the prepared pan and pat evenly onto the bottom of the pan.

Bake until golden brown, about 12 minutes. Let cool in the pan on a wire rack. Leave the oven set at 350°F [180°C].

CONT'D

MEANWHILE, MAKE THE TOPPING: In a saucepan over low heat, heat the butter until it melts and bubbles. Add the dark brown sugar, honey, cream, and maple syrup and bring to a boil over medium heat, stirring constantly. Let the mixture boil without stirring for 1 minute.

Pour the topping over the crust, tilting the pan to distribute evenly, and sprinkle the nuts over the top.

Return the pan to the oven and bake until the caramel layer is bubbly all over, 12 to 15 minutes. Remove the pan from the oven and sprinkle with the chocolate chips, distributing them evenly over the top. Set the pan aside and let the chocolate chips melt for 1 to 2 minutes, then swirl the chocolate with a spatula to create a wavelike pattern in the topping.

Set the pan on the wire rack and let rest until the bars are completely cool. Invert the baking pan onto the rack. Lift off the parchment paper and discard. Place a cutting board on the bars and invert again. Cut into 1½-by-2-in [4-by-5-cm] bars.

Store layered between sheets of wax paper in an airtight container for up to 1 week.

MAKES ABOUT 40 BARS

BONBONS

12 oz [360 g] dark chocolate, finely chopped

1½ cups [360 ml] heavy cream

½ cup [50 g] premium unsweetened cocoa powder

Place the chocolate in a mixing bowl.

In a small saucepan over medium heat, heat the cream just until you see steam rising from the center and tiny bubbles forming around the edges of the pan.

Slowly pour the hot cream over the chocolate and let stand, without stirring, for 4 minutes. With a rubber spatula, gently stir just until smooth and the chocolate is fully melted. Do not stir quickly or you will incorporate air bubbles.

Drape a paper towel over the bowl and cover with plastic wrap. Refrigerate until the chocolate is firm and scoopable, 4 hours or up to overnight.

Place the cocoa powder in a soup bowl or other shallow container.

Using a small ice-cream scoop, scoop the chocolate into 1½-in [4-cm] balls, dropping them into the cocoa powder and gently rolling the balls around until they are well coated. Transfer the bonbons to a serving plate. Repeat until all the chocolate has been used.

Store in an airtight container in the refrigerator for up to 1 week. Serve at room temperature.

MAKES 24 BONBONS

BANGKOK MARGARITA

2 oz [60 ml] Reposado tequila

2 oz [60 ml] pineapple juice

1 oz [30 ml] Domaine de Canton
ginger liqueur

Pinch of Maldon sea salt

Pinch of Aleppo pepper

1 lime

Combine the tequila, pineapple juice, and ginger liqueur in a cocktail shaker filled with ice. Shake and strain into a martini glass. Sprinkle the salt and pepper on top. With a Microplane grater, grate the zest of the lime over the top of the drink. Tap the grater lightly to release the zest and oil into the drink.
    Serve immediately.

SERVES 1

41

CLASSIC MARTINI

3 oz [90 ml] Boodles gin

2 dashes vermouth

1 rosemary sprig or 1 pimiento-stuffed green olive

Fill a 5-oz [150-ml] martini glass with ice and set aside for several minutes to chill. Combine the gin and vermouth in a cocktail shaker filled with ice. Shake vigorously. Empty the ice from the martini glass. Strain the drink into the chilled glass and garnish with the rosemary.

Serve immediately.

SERVES 1

43

THE
BIG O

4 or 5 fresh raspberries

2 oz [60 ml] premium vodka

1 to 2 oz [30 to 60 ml] chilled Champagne

In a bowl, muddle the raspberries until they are mashed to a fine purée. Transfer to a small, shallow bowl. Dip the rim of a chilled cocktail glass into the raspberry purée. Carefully add the vodka without disturbing the prepared rim. Pour in the Champagne so that it floats on top.

Serve immediately.

SERVES 1

45

THE
BLOOD ORANGE

1 blood orange wedge, 1 blood
orange wheel, and 1½ oz [45 ml]
fresh blood orange juice

Superfine sugar for coating

1½ oz [45 ml] orange vodka

¼ oz [10 ml] Mandarine Napoléon
or other orange liqueur

¼ oz [10 ml] Lillet Blanc

Drop of orange flower water

Rub the rim of a large chilled cocktail glass with the orange wedge
and dip in the sugar to coat. Combine the vodka, orange juice,
orange liqueur, Lillet Blanc, and orange flower water in a cocktail
shaker filled with ice. Shake vigorously, then strain into the
prepared glass and garnish with the orange wheel.

Serve immediately.

SERVES 1

47

CHAMPAGNE COCKTAIL

1 sugar cube

4 dashes Angostura bitters

4 oz [120 ml] dry Champagne

1 lemon twist

Put the sugar cube in a 6-oz [180-ml] Champagne flute. Sprinkle all sides of the sugar cube with the bitters. Gradually add the Champagne to the flute and garnish with the lemon twist.
Serve immediately.

SERVES 1

49

APPLETINI

¼ cup [35 g] peeled, diced apple, or 1 oz [30 ml] apple juice, plus 1 thin apple slice

¼ oz [10 ml] fresh lemon juice

1½ oz [45 ml] good-quality vodka or apple vodka

½ oz [15 ml] green apple schnapps

Muddle the diced apple and lemon juice in the bottom of a cocktail shaker. Add ice, the vodka, and schnapps to the shaker. Shake vigorously, strain into a chilled cocktail glass, and garnish with the apple slice, placed on the rim.

Serve immediately.

SERVES 1

SAZERAC

½ oz [15 ml] Pernod liqueur

1 sugar cube

3 dashes Peychaud's aromatic bitters

3 oz [90 ml] rye whiskey

1 lemon twist

Fill a 5-oz [150-ml] martini glass with ice and set aside for several minutes to chill. Empty the ice from the glass and add the Pernod. Coat the inside of the glass with the Pernod by gently rotating the stem of the glass in full circles. Empty the Pernod from the glass.

Put the sugar cube in a cocktail shaker and coat the cube thoroughly with the bitters. Cover with a handful of ice and add the whiskey. Muddle the ingredients thoroughly until the ice is slushy. Shake vigorously for 10 seconds, strain into the prepared martini glass, and garnish with the lemon twist.

Serve immediately.

SERVES 1

THE
FIERY ALMOND

1 Tbsp amaretto, plus ¾ oz [20 ml]

1 Tbsp cocoa powder

½ Tbsp chipotle powder

½ oz [15 ml] Kahlúa

1 oz [30 ml] light cream or half-and-half

Moisten the rim of an old-fashioned glass with the 1 Tbsp amaretto. Combine the cocoa powder and chipotle powder on a small plate. Roll the rim of the glass in the mixture to coat.

Fill the prepared glass halfway with ice. Add the remaining ¾ oz [20 ml] amaretto and the Kahlúa to a cocktail shaker along with a handful of ice. Shake and then strain into the prepared glass. Gently pour the cream into the drink over the back of a spoon to create a cream float on top without disturbing the rest of the drink.

Serve immediately.

SERVES 1

55

THE
PINK GRAPEFRUIT

SIMPLE SYRUP

1 cup [240 ml] water

1 cup [100 g] sugar

Crushed pink peppercorns
for coating

½ large grapefruit, peeled and
separated into segments

2 oz [60 ml] rum

Splash of grenadine

TO MAKE THE SIMPLE SYRUP: Combine the water and sugar in a
small saucepan. Bring to a boil, continuously stirring until the
sugar dissolves. Once the water starts to boil, lower the heat and
let simmer, uncovered, for 10 minutes. Remove from the heat and
let cool to room temperature. The syrup can be stored in a glass
container in the refrigerator for up to 1 week.

Moisten the rim of a cocktail glass with 1 Tbsp simple syrup.
Place the peppercorns on a small plate. Roll the rim of the glass in
the peppercorns to coat.

In a cocktail shaker, muddle the grapefruit segments with 1 oz
[30 ml] simple syrup. Add a handful of ice, and pour in the rum.
Shake and then strain into the prepared glass. Add the grenadine
(just enough to give the drink a rosy pink tint).

Serve immediately.

SERVES 1

57

HOT
CHOCOLATE

1 qt [960 ml] 2% or whole milk

1 cup [180 g] chopped milk chocolate

2 Tbsp unsweetened cocoa powder, plus more for serving

Whipped cream or marshmallows

Bring the milk to a simmer in a medium saucepan over medium to medium-high heat. Add the chocolate and cocoa powder. Whisk until the chocolate has melted. Simmer for an additional 1 minute, whisking continuously. Remove from the heat and pour into mugs.

Serve topped with dollops of whipped cream and a sprinkle of cocoa powder.

SERVES 4

CRANBERRY CORNUCOPIA

5 cups [1.2 L] water

12 cranberry-apple tea bags

1 cup [400 g] brown sugar

2½ cups [600 ml] cranberry juice

12 whole star anise

Zest of 1 orange, cut into strips

4 cups [960 ml] strained orange juice

3½ cups [840 ml] spiced rum

12 lemon slices

Bring the water to a boil in a large saucepan. Remove from the heat, add the tea bags, and cover. Steep for 5 minutes.

Remove the tea bags and add the brown sugar, cranberry juice, star anise, and orange zest. Bring the mixture to a boil over medium-high heat. Lower the heat and simmer for 10 minutes. Add the orange juice and rum and stir until warm. Remove from the heat and strain, reserving the star anise.

Serve ladled into mugs, garnished with the star anise and lemon slices.

SERVES 12

WASSAIL BOWL

GARNISH

6 small to medium apples

2 Tbsp brown sugar

1 tsp ground cinnamon

MULLED CIDER

9 cups [2.1 L] amber ale

2 cups [480 ml] sweet sherry

1½ cups [300 g] firmly packed brown sugar

6 whole cloves

6 whole allspice berries

1 cinnamon stick

1½ tsp ground ginger

¾ tsp ground nutmeg

TO MAKE THE GARNISH: Preheat the oven to 350°F [180°C]. Core the apples and place them in a small baking pan. Combine the brown sugar and cinnamon in a small bowl and fill each apple with 1 tsp of the mixture. Add water to cover the bottom of the pan and bake until the apples are soft, about 30 minutes. Remove from the oven and set aside to cool. When the apples are cool enough to handle, cut two of them into thin slices. Set aside.

TO MAKE THE MULLED CIDER: Combine the ale, sherry, brown sugar, and all the spices in a large saucepan and simmer over medium heat for 15 minutes. Remove from the heat, strain, and discard the solids.

Serve the cider in a wassail bowl or punch bowl, floating the whole baked apples on top. Ladle into mugs and garnish each with an apple slice.

SERVES 12